In the Holy Land
Paintings by David Roberts
1839

Wolfgang Schuler

STUDIO
EDITIONS

The pictures were kindly lent to the publishers
by private owners

Translated by S. Bollinger

Cover:
A view across the Kidron Valley to the Temple Mount
with the Dome of the Rock and the El-Aqsa mosque (front)

Nazareth, Mary's Well (back)

First published in 1991 by Steimatzky Ltd,
Bnei Brak, Israel

Copyright © 1991 by I. P. Verlagsgesellschaft
International Publishing GmbH, Munich, Germany

This 1995 edition published by Studio Editions Ltd,
Princess House, 50 Eastcastle Street,
London W 1 N 7AP, England

Bethlehem   Holy Land – much contested land

«The incorrigible tourists have arrived, their pockets full of bits of stone they have chipped off ruins. I wish a stop could be put to this vandalism. They have broken bits off Noah's tomb, off the delightful paintings in the temple of Baalbek, off the houses of Judas and Ananias in Damascus, off the tomb of Nimrod,the great hunter, off the faded Greek and Roman inscriptions on the ancient, grey walls of Banja's castle and now they have hacked and scraped these old arches which Jesus once looked on. May Heaven protect the Holy Sepulchre when these hordes hit Jerusalem». These were the words of Mark Twain who, in his capacity as a journalist, journeyed through the Mediterranean countries in 1867 and reported from Palestine, the Holy Land, the destination of pilgrims from three world religions wishing to visit their holy sites – Jews, Christians and followers of Islam. These pious Europeans usually landed in Jaffa, today Tel Aviv. A French traveller writes at the end of the 18th century: «Jaffa is the place where the pilgrims land. They come here in November and make straight for Jerusalem, where they remain until Easter.» And: «. . . . you land in Jaffa together with the rice sent from Danietta (on the right arm of the Nile in Lower Egypt) to Jerusalem and the goods for a small French shop opened in Ramle and with the pilgrims from Morea (Peleponese) and from Constantinople and with the foodstuffs from the Syrian coast; it is also from this port that the cotton spun in the whole of Palestine and the foodstuffs which Palestine exports leave the country.» Moritz Busch from Dresden described, in 1861, the scene which met the eyes of the new arrivals and which must have seem loud, colourful and

3

slightly exotic to people from Central and Western Europe: Here «a group of local Fellaheen (peasants) are arguing loudly and gesticulating wildly about a goat or a sheep», and there «squat sellers of garlic and oranges, onions and cucumbers in their turbans... camels and donkeys are being sheared, loaded and unloaded. Kavass and Bashibazouks, Negroes and Bedouins, garments as black as coal and as white as snow, red fezes, white, blue and green turbans, red and yellow shoes with pointed toes and naked feet all throng together. Mukarin (mule drovers) and grooms show off their animals to potential buyers or people wanting to hire them, riding them so that their manes and tails fly in the wind.»

Strangers have come to this land since time immemorial, have passed through or have settled. And it has always been a land which was fought over, a bone of contention and more or less easy prey for neighbouring powers: Babylon, Egypt, the Hittite empire, Assyria, Persia, it was conquered by Alexander the Great, later by Rome, came under Byzantine administration and was overrun by Islamic Arabs.

It was in this land that the oldest known town in the world was excavated, Jericho, which is at least nine thousand years old. Its walls are said to have fallen to the children of Israel in the thirteenth century before Christ at the sound of Joshua's trumpets, Joshua being the successor of Moses: «For when the people heard the trumpets echoing they let out a great shout. And the walls fell down and the children of Israel climbed straight into the town. And so they took the town» – which is, in fact, merely a legend as Jericho had already been destroyed in 1550 BC by an Egyptian army and remained uninhabited for almost a thousand years.

Towards the end of the second millenium non-Semitic Philistines settled in the southern part of the country. Their five most important towns were Gaza, Ashkelon, Ashdod, Ekron and Gath. The Philistines had probably come from the Aegean islands or from Crete. They gave their name to the whole of the country – in Hebrew: Pelistim –, for the Romans called the province Palestina after the last Jewish rebellion against Rome (131–35 AD) in order to erase the memory of the old name of Judea and replace it with that of the Jews' arch enemies. The Jews were no longer allowed to enter the Holy City of Jerusalem and the surrounding area on penalty of death. After the period of exile in Babylon during the sixth century, during which many lives were lost, and after the destruction of the temple in Jerusalem first by the neo-Babylonian King Nebuchadnezzer II and then by the Romans this was the final blow which caused the Jews to migrate over the whole of the ancient world. And those who remained in Palestine under Roman and then Byzantine rule were forced finally to succumb to the onslaught of the Arabs in 634, as were the other countries of the Middle East, North Africa and finally even Spain.

Arab dynasties ruled over the country for the next nine hundred years except for the period of the crusader states in the Middle Ages, a period of some two hundred years, until the Osmanic Turks seized the country in 1516. This Turkish occupation lasted four hundred years and only ended with the First World War.

4

In the Sinaite Mountains

Napoleon's Egyptian expedition in 1799, aimed against England, had taken some of the French troops into the Holy Land as well, so that it became a centre of European colonial interest. Napoleon's Egyptian campaign came to an end when he failed to take the stronghold of Akko, north of Haifa. He is quoted as saying: «It is not worth wasting even a couple of days to take the fortress of Akko. The brave men I might lose in such an undertaking are needed for more important operations.» An eye-witness who took part in the campaign said, on the other hand: «We had no form of transport and had a thousand or even twelve hundred wounded and sick men with us, quite apart from forty pieces of artillery... All the rest, canons of all varieties, mortars, grenades, bombs, muskets, bullets had to be buried in the fields or on the beach... Everything was ready for withdrawal when the enemy lauched an attack on 20. May; it lasted the whole day. The fire was dreadful. The enemy went on attacking our trenches but Reynier's division was successful in fighting them off, although only with great loss of life». The French withdrew to Egypt leaving a scorched earth behind them: «The towns, villages, hamlets and the rich harvest that covered the land were like so many torches along our way, once we had set fire to them».

Many years later a traveller to the Holy Land wrote about the scars left by such devastation: «The municipal gardens were formerly ravaged by the infamous Abu Dahab, more recently by Bonaparte, by Djezzar Pasha and twice by Pasha Abu Marrak. They are now just beginning to bloom again as the vegetation is faster

5

here. I visited the garden of a Christian, which he had just replanted and which he assured me had once brought him 2000 piastres a year. It was irrigated by means of a water wheel, like all the other gardens.»

For centuries before Napoleon's campaign the visitors from Europe had mainly been Christian pilgrims who saw the country through the eyes of men familiar with the Bible but this changed, Napoleon brought a whole team of scholars with him. The result of this military expedition as far as scholarship was concerned was the famous Description de l'Egypte, which appeared between 1809 and 1822, with many illustrations such as no other previous work had had and which presented a hitherto unknown world to the Europeans and paved the way for Egyptology as a field. Amongst the antiquities which were collected was the Stone of Rosetta, which was inscribed in two languages and three types of writing and which enabled Jean-Francois Champollion to decipher the hieroglyphics in 1922. It was also a French officer who first made an official survey of Palestine, above all the coastline, and drew up the first useful map of the country to a scale of 1:100 000.

Real scientific exploration of this part of the world only began, however, with the American scholar and professor of theology Edward Robinson, who walked all around Egypt, the Sinai peninsula and Palestine in 1838, the same year as David Roberts arrived in Alexandria. Robinson published the geographical results of his expedition in the form of a diary in 1841: *Biblical researches in Palestine and the adjacent countries*. He personally supervised and

Sea of Galilee with Tiberias

6

Nablus   authorized the German translation, which appeared in three volumes the same year in Halle: *Palästina und die südlich angrenzenden Länder. Tagebuch einer Reise im Jahre 1838 in Bezug auf die biblische Geographie unternommen von E. Robinson und E. Smith* (Palestine and the adjacent countries to the South. A diary of a journey made in 1838 with reference to the geography of the Bible by E. Robinson and E. Smith.)

Alexandria, which in those days was the main port and the most important trading town in Egypt, a vassall state of Turkey, was a second port from which sea-voyagers could enter the Holy Land after Palestine's own port of Jaffa, which could only take small ships. The journey across the Sinai peninsula was, however, difficult and dangerous. Robinson describes the impression this strange world made on him as follows: «As soon as we had set foot on land we needed no more proof that we had left Europe and were now in the Orient. We found ourselves in the middle of a huge crowd through which we could only make a way for ourselves with great difficulty; we were surrounded by Egyptians, Turks, Arabs, Copts, Negroes and Franks (Europeans); white people, black people, people with olive-coloured skins, light and dark brown skins and many other colours; men with long beards and men with no beards; national costumes of all kinds and no costumes at all; silk and rags; wide, flowing robes and nakedness; women hidden in formless black robes, their faces completely covered so that only their eyes peeped out through two small holes; endless confusion and chattering, a mixture of lan-

Petra – Arabs' Consultation

guages, Arabic, Turkish, Greek, Italian, French, German and English, depending on where you were; long lines of gigantic camels, one behind the other with huge loads on their backs; little donkeys, harnessed and saddled, and each led by an Arab boy with wicked eyes who chattered away at you in broken English and managed to get his donkey between your legs whether you wanted it or not.»

Robinson also tells us in detail about the difficulties a traveller from Europe faced in the Orient: «The traveller certainly knows the moment he lands in Alexandria that he has stepped into the Orient and he is again reminded of the fact when he sets about leaving the town . . . .So far he has had all the comforts on his travels which are available in Europe and America; he merely had to wait for the steamer to sail and go on board with all his luggage, without giving a thought to anything or having to worry about anything. But travelling in Egypt and Syria is quite different. Here the traveller will find neither asphalted roads nor guards nor inns and is therefore left to his own devices. In Egypt he has to hire a boat for himself unless he finds a companion to share it with him; he has to take his own bed, cooking utensils and food with him on his journey except for those things he can get in the villages along the Nile; above all he needs a servant who can function as a cook, provider of food and interpreter at the same time. He will soon find himself completely in the power of this important person, who can usually neither read

nor write; and the unpleasantness and problems of this dependence will continue to plague him until he learns some Arabic himself or is fortunate enough (as was the case with me) to meet a companion who knows the language well. If the traveller has the time he would be well advised to buy most of what he needs in Alexandria. He will need these things just as much on the way to Cairo as afterwards and this will save him time and the worry of finding them in Cairo.»

Robinson had arrived in Alexandria on 30. December, 1837. Nine months later, on 24. September, 1838, David Roberts, a painter of landscapes and architecture from Scotland, arrived in the Egyptian port. His work of several magnificent volumes «The Holy Land, Syria, Idumea, Arabia, Egypt and Nubia» with lithographs, appeared 1842 to 1849, made him famous and presented the European and American public with the most beautiful views of the best known regions.

On the track of the Bible

David Roberts was the son of a cobbler and was born on 24. October 1796 in Stockbridge near Edinburgh. He grew up in extremely poor surroundings. His unusual artistic talent began to show itself from a very early age; he would cover the walls of the

kitchen of his parents' home with animal scenes in red chalk to show
his mother the exciting things he had seen on the advertising boards
of wandering circusses and menageries. At the same time they
awakened his curiosity about foreign countries and whetted his
appetite for adventure.

Going down into the Jordan Valley

As his parents' miserable financial situation made any better form
of training impossible he worked for seven years as an apprentice
painter and decorator after he left school. At home he drew and
painted from Nature and what is more, he did this with such skill as
to deceive the eye. He once scared the life out of his mother, who
was leafing through his portfolio, with a copy of a one-pound note.
Such a banknote was seldom seen in this poor family and David had
never seen one until one day his master gave him one to pay a
merchant; the merchant was not at home when David called so he
had plenty of time to copy the banknote, which he found very
attractive. This made his mother think for a minute that he was a
thief.

In 1816 he began to work as a scene-painter with a wandering
circus to which a small pantomime theatre was attached. «That was
the height of my ambition,» he wrote later, «for my idea of art had
been picked up mainly from the stage of the Edinburgh Theatre
seen from the shilling gallery.» He was, for example, thrilled by the
set for «Ali Baba and the Forty Thieves» which had captivated him
with its oriental magic: «Bagdad with its countless minarets was

10

Samaria   quite familiar to me and there was scarcely a single night when, on my return from the theatre, I didn't make a sketch of what I had seen.» In those days he could not imagine that he would one day travel through the Orient himself and paint and draw, on the spot, those views which give a much more exact picture of the world of the Middle East than the romantic rubbish printed in the programme of the Edinburgh Theatre.

His unsettled life with the circus and pantomime theatre, in which he sometimes had to help out as an actor, may not have seemed to be the beginning of a serious career, especially since the members of such a circus tended to be regarded as vagabonds, but Roberts was happy: He was able to travel around and paint and get to know the work of other scene painters. His early work as a painter in the circus even influenced his later works, especially those from the Orient, as they usually have that characteristic dramatic touch in the treatment of the rocks, mountains, buildings and the light effect which was so typical of stage sets in those days.

In York he had plenty of time to draw and paint: «It is only here that I have become a real painter...I've spent hours sitting in the snow drawing the minster...this has been my only primer on Gothic architecture...day after day I spent drawing every buttress, every baldachin, every bit of tracery, every crocket (a Gothic form of ornamentation in the form of a clover leaf) with the utmost care, with all the passion and admiration of a first love...Did I not even

11

climb to the top of a monument to stand for a whole hour on one leg drawing the rich tracery on Bishop Greenwood's grave?...Is there an old abbey or village church within a twelve mile radius that I haven't visited?»

In January 1817 the troop of actors was back in Edinburgh and broke up in May. Robert's career as a scene painter took him to the following theatres in the next few years: 1819 to the Royal Theatre in Glasgow, 1820 to the Royal Theatre in Edinburgh, 1822 to Drury Lane Theatre in London and 1826 to Covent Garden. He was successful and became well known. The Times wrote about one of Robert's sets: «That was a tremendous task for one single person but it was executed in a way which marks Roberts as a genius of unusual talent.» And another newspaper commented: «This is without exception the finest set we have ever seen in a theatre. It includes a series of magnificent, first-class paintings .. all by Roberts, now lost to Drury Lane...» During this period he was involved in the founding of the Society of British Artists, of which he was to become president in 1831. And in 1824 his first painting , «Dryburgh Abbey», was shown in the British Institution.

In 1820 he had married Margaret McLachlan. The marriage was not a happy one and broke up after only a few years. In spite of his work, and later his journeys, he was always a loving and devoted father to the only child of this marriage, his daughter Christine, with whom he developed a very close relationship.

His first journey to the European mainland brought him success as a painter of buildings: in 1825 he sold several paintings with views of Gothic churches in Dieppe and Rouen, works which The Times also praised. His next journey to the Continent took him to Holland and Germany, up the Rhine as far as Mannheim and Heidelberg, where he greatly admired the castle: «This wonderful castle...the finest remnant of Germany's greatness...destroyed and empty...there was a song in the air...about the sad ghosts that wander through the decayed halls of the old gloomy caverns in the castle of Heidelberg.»

In 1832 there followed a long journey to Spain, where he draw and painted buildings and ruins from Antiquity, the Arabian period, the Middle Ages and the Renaissance. In 1837 a selection of these appeared under the title: Picturesque Sketches in Spain. After only two months, 1200 copies at four guineas each had already been sold, although Roberts never saw much of the money as the publisher had cheated him.

Even as a child Roberts had dreamed of one day visiting the countries which had been the scene of events in the Bible. Now he could afford such a journey. A journey which was to make him famous. He prepared for it very carefully, collecting all the information he could find about the countries and the people, their customs and their culture, the political and social situation; he also equipped himself with various letters of recommendation from the British Foreign Minister to the Consuls in Egypt and Syria and other influential people.

He travelled via Paris, down the Rhone valley to Marseilles, where he arrived on 11. September, 1838. He took a passage on the

Pilgrims being baptized in the River Jordan, in the foreground the Governor of Jerusalem and his guard

steamship «Dante» and continued his journey in stormy weather to Civitavecchia, where he stepped for the first time on to Italian soil: «It is a tormenting thought, to be only ten hours' journey from the Eternal City.» Six days later he reached Malta and changed ships there. On one of the Cyclades, perhaps Siros, he changed ships again; on board there were Turkish pilgrims on their way to Mecca: «Of course, I quickly got out my sketch book. They cast themselves on the deck and prayed six or seven times a day . . . a most impressive sight.»

On 24. September, after two weeks at sea, Roberts arrived in Alexandria: «Our ship was surrounded by a teeming mass of little boats, the men in them rowing, shoving and shouting in their attempts to catch passengers. And it became even more exciting when we disembarked: there was such jostling and fighting for the luggage among the poor black porters that it was hard to keep an eye on one's cases. For the sake of a couple of halfpennies they were willing to put up with all the pushing and knocking.» This was how he described his arrival in the Orient in a letter to his daughter Christine.

Roberts was greeted by the same colourful, noisy activity that Edward Robinson had described so well. He was horrified at the slave market: Beautiful Circassian girls, greatly valued in the harems of the Osmanic Empire, were decked out in finery but the young African girls crouched, almost naked, on the ground «in sunshine

which would have killed a European, a dreadful sight,» he wrote to his daughter, «and I felt proud to belong to a nation that had abolished slavery.»

The Convent of Mar Saba in the Judaean Desert between Jerusalem and the Dead Sea

Roberts travelled around Egypt first. For three months he and a couple of other British travellers hired a boat to sail down the Nile and the first thing he did was to put it completely under water to get rid of the rats that were everywhere. The boat cost fifteen pounds a month to hire, including pay for the crew, which consisted of eight Egyptians and Nubians. For some of the time they were accompanied by a second boat, also with Englishmen on board. Their adventurous voyage took them as far as Abu Simbel in Nubia, which they reached on 8. November. Roberts was greatly impressed by the ever changing scenery: small villages among palm trees in the narrow strips of fertile land, the houses made of bricks of Nile mud dried in the sun, groups of women with their children, washing clothes in the river or fetching water, Fellaheen walking or riding donkeys along the riverbank, the tall triangular sails of the feluccas dominating the river scene and then more patches of desert which reached right down to the river, particularly between Luxor and Assuan, and now and again the islands with their luxurious vegetation.

They spent several days at the most important sites, where Roberts painted or drew the ancient Egyptian monuments, usually making several sketches in various different lights. Towards the end

14

Hebron

of the journey he forgot his sketch book containing drawings of Nubia in a cave he visited on a trip ashore and only realized what had happened 80 miles further up the Nile. It took days to get the invaluable material back.

On 21. December he was back in Cairo with more than a hundred drawings and paintings: «I am the first artist, at least from England, to have been here. I know now that the works of the French artists give no idea of these wonderful remains...»

He stayed for two weeks in Egypt's capital, walking all round the old quarters and the immediate surroundings of the city drawing pictures. He was probably the first European to receive permission to enter mosques and paint and draw what he saw inside – a rare privilege for a Christian traveller even during the next few decades. One of the conditions for this privilege was that he should not use a brush made of pigs' bristles and he also had to dress in local costume: «Before I was allowed to enter the mosque I had to draw my whiskers over my upper lip and dress completely in Arab costume. On these conditions I was allowed to make sketches in both oils and water colours of the main mosque.»

In Cairo he met two Englishmen, John Pell and John G. Kinnear, who were also on their way to Syria (in those days Syria was the name given to the whole of the area between the Mediterranean and the River Euphrates, between Asia Minor in the North and the Arabian peninsula and Egypt in the south). They decided to travel

15

together and immediately began to make the necessary preparations.

They set off on 7. February, 1839. The group consisted of eight people, the travellers and their armed servants, all wearing Arab or Turkish costumes. They were also accompanied by Hanafi Ismail Effendi, a Christian from Egypt with whom Roberts had become friendly in Cairo; Effendi had spent several years in England, had converted to Christianity in Glasgow and was now in charge of a factory. He spoke fluent English and was, of course, very familiar with the conditions to be expected on their travels. Their 21 camels, which also carried the provisions, tents and luggage, and the fifteen Bedouins under Sheich Hussein, who made up their escort, formed a regular small caravan. They crossed Suez and set off in the direction of Mount Sinai. The journey was a difficult one, particularly for Western Europeans.

Kinnear published the letters he sent to his family in Scotland in a book in 1841: *Cairo, Petra and Damascus, in 1839,* which he dedicated to Roberts. In the dedication at the beginning of the book he writes: «My dear Roberts ... I may hope that you will find here and there some few words of conversation with our old friend Sheich Hussein or some little incident ... which shall recall to your mind scenes which could not be made the subject of your art.»

In a letter dated 14. February Kinnear writes about the inhospitable landscape in the Western Sinai: «We had now left the more open part of the Desert, and our route lay among narrow sandy valleys,

Resting on the way to the Sinai Desert

between rugged precipitous crags of calcareous rock, mixed with beds of gravel and indurated sand. You can hardly imagine a more savage scene. The crags rose sometimes perpendicularly, like enormous walls, their summits riven and shattered into the most wild and fantastic forms; occasionally the valleys opened out wider, and high isolated masses of rock rose abruptly from the sand, curiously turreted and embattled, and having their naked sides worn and undermined by the drifting sand, as if they had been subjected to the action of a torrent. Nature has often been represented as smiling; here she might be said to wear a ghastly and frantic grin. No living thing was to be seen, except the little grey lizards that darted across our path, or lay basking in the burning sunshine on the stones: the air was hot and motionless, and the glare from the white rocks and sand became painful to the eyes. For the first time I began to feel the thirst rather distressing, and the water, being heated by the sun, and having already acquired a nauseous taste from the skins, afforded little refreshment. How little do we think, in reading the history of Israel's wanderings in the wilderness, of the trials and temptations to which they were exposed.»

After ten days they reached the Convent of St. Catherine at the foot of Moses' mountain. According to the legend God is supposed to have appeared to Moses in a burning bush at this spot. The convent was inhabited by old Greek monks, who made the exhausted travellers welcome. Getting into the convent was, however, quite a dangerous business. By means of a rope with a loop at the end of it the Europeans were pulled up to a window some ten feet above them whereby the person being hauled up had to use his feet to avoid collision with the rough projections of the wall. As Arabs were not allowed into the convent a bundle of twigs was thrown down to the Muslim escort so that they could make a fire while the Christians were given a meagre meal. Roberts: «There was pilaf and dried dates and never have poor pilgrims slept as well as I did under the hospitable roof of the monks of St. Catherine.» Perhaps this had something to do with the arrack, which Kinnear praises in his book and which the abbot offers them in a «curious old flask of gilded crystal.»

They spent four nights in the convent and went on excursions into the Sinaite mountains and to the summit of Moses' mountain, the Mount Horeb of the Bible, where Jahve is said to have handed Moses the tablet on which the Ten Commandments were written. The steep ascent was difficult and dangerous for the upper reaches, out of the sun, were slippery with ice and snow. Kinnear spent a long

Ascent of Mount Sinai

Gulf of Akaba with a small island and the ruins of a crusader castle

time in his book wondering whether this really could be the Horeb of the Bible and came to the conclusion that it must have been a different mountain because of details mentioned in the Bible and geographical details; more recent Bible scholars have confirmed this, in fact.

During these four days Roberts finished at least eight drawings of the old convent, some of the individual buildings, Moses' mountain, the summit and the ascent to the summit.

The caravan set off again on 22. February, provided with bread, dates and rice from the convent's store-cupboard. Days later they reached the Gulf of Akaba, where the fresh breeze was very welcome in the heat. Soon, however, the wind blew up into a veritable sandstorm which caused them a great deal of discomfort when they had to pitch their tents in the evening. Kinnear described the scene as follows: «Our eyes, noses and ears were filled with sand; quite a lot of it had got into one of my portmanteaus which contained provisions. The water, too, was worse than ever; stinking and full of animalcules, and I could scarcely swallow it after being strained through two or three pocket-handkerchiefs.»

They arrived in Akaba, hungry and thirsty, on 27. February. Akaba was a sleepy little place consisting of a fortress, for the protection of pilgrims on the annual pilgrimage to Mecca, and a few meagre hovels. Some three thousand years previously, King Solomon had stationed his fleet here to secure the flourishing trade with Southern Arabia and East Africa. And the ancient city of Elath, near Akaba or even on the same site, the port of the Edomites and in

19

Petra, centre right-the tents of Roberts and his companions

the possession of the Jews under David and Solomon, had still been an important trading centre under Byzantine and Roman rule and later, during the crusades, the crusader knights and the Muslims fought many a battle over it. There was nothing left to remind one of this glorious past. Roberts did not find a single boat and it was a mystery to him what the people lived on.

In Akaba their old escort under Sheich Hussein turned back as this was as far as their authority went; a new escort from a different Bedouin tribe was to accompany them from now on but the new escort did not arrive for three days, which meant they were held up and very annoyed at having to waste time in such an ugly, depressing place; the only relief they had were their walks to the Gulf of an afternoon, followed by a refreshing dip in the sea.

When the new escort finally arrived they had to negotiate the price for the journey via Petra to Hebron, in addition to all their other problems. The result of the negotiations was not very satisfactory: 4500 piastres, about forty-five pounds. In spite of their dissatisfaction they celebrated their agreement with a banquet about which the new sheich said he'd had many a good meal, but never one quite like this: «El-ham-dulillah!»

They continued their journey next day through Wady Araba, a wide, dry river-bed between the Gulf of Akaba and the Dead Sea. After many exciting adventures, which did not do a great deal to strengthen their faith in their new Arab escort, they reached the old

20

Petra, eastern end of the valley

Nabatic capital of Petra in the narrow valley of the upper part of the Wady Mousa, which is difficult of access, a region which was known for its wild, thieving inhabitants.

The men were completely overwhelmed at the sight of the town hewn in the red sandstone. Kinnear writes: «It is certainly one of the most wonderful scenes in the world. The eye wanders in amazement from the stupendous rampart of rocks which surrounds the valley to the porticoes and ornamented doorways sculptured on its surface. The dark yawning entrances of the temples and tombs, and the long ranges of excavated chambers, give an air of emptiness and desolation to the scene, which I cannot well describe. . . . But in the valley itself, the patches of green corn among the ruins, the stream bordered with oleander and willow, the sweet sound of the running water, and the cry of the cuckoo and the partridge, were all delightful and refreshing after the silence and dreary solitude of the Desert.»

During the next few days they got to know the old town better. It was situated at what had been the point at which the caravan routes from the North to the South and the East to the West had crossed and was therefore an important trading centre. Petra was only rediscovered in 1812 by a Swiss researcher Johann Ludwig Burckhardt. The place was so far away from civilization, almost enchanted, that Kinnear was reminded of the prophecy with regard to Edom: «. . . will lie waste, none shall pass through it for ever . . . and thorns

will grow in the palaces, nettles and briars in the fortresses; and it will be a home for the jackals . . . .» The travellers' stay in Petra was also unsettled and uneasy. They had to negotiate with the local inhabitants about permission to visit the ancient sites. The leader of their escort also turned out to be everything but reliable, he even seemed to be hand-in-glove with the local big-wigs. There was nothing unusual about sudden confrontations with grim-faced, armed Arabs, who seemed to appear from nowhere – in fact it was quite the order of the day. There was thieving and one night they even caught a thief in the act of stealing but he was able to escape in the darkness. There was even a regular attack on the party when a group of Arabs with long muskets rushed out at them from behind rocks and bushes, shouting and gesticulating wildly. They had a narrow escape, in fact, as the robbers were only interested in the money a local sheich had just collected from the them as a toll. Very much to the amazement of the travellers the sheich then held court over one of the party of robbers, at their request, who was accused of having stolen a donkey – a scene which Roberts drew, of course, Arabs' Consultation – in short, the Arab way of life remained a mystery to the European observers.

22

They continued their journey on 11. March, first passing Mount Hor, where Aaron is said to be buried. As their Arab escort was very eager to leave this region as quickly as possible they decided against climbing up to Aaron's Tomb. After several other adventurous incidents and dangerous meetings the group of travellers reached Hebron on 15. March. Beautifully situated on the slope of a hill, surrounded by vineyards and olive groves, Hebron was a picturesque sight. Four thousand people lived there, among then forty Jewish families and one Christian household. The Muslims of Hebron had the reputation of being bigoted and fanatical: «We found that it would be useless, if not dangerous, to attempt to enter their mosque.» This mosque, originally a Byzantine church, is said to be built over the cave of Machpelah and houses the tombs of Abraham, Sarah, Isaac, Rebecca, Jacob and Leah, revered by Jews and Muslims alike.

As the plague was in Jerusalem and anyone leaving the Holy City had to reckon with forty days' quarantine, they decided for the time being to go to Gaza. The plague also seemed to have claimed victims in Hebron, although nothing had been announced officially. It was merely noticeable that there were an increasing number of burials and groups of «mourning women» were to be seen in the street. «Groups of females, enveloped in their long, white veils were all day seated among the tombs, screaming and slapping their faces, or sitting in mournful silence by the new graves.»

Gaza with troops (right) on the way to Sidon

The road to Gaza took them through very fertile country. They rode through cornfields and cultivated pastures and olive-plantations. There was, however, evidence of a great deal of neglect, the system of husbandry was imperfect; large portions of land lay uncultivated, covered in luxuriant, wild vegetation. The houses in the small villages bore witness to the long and rich history of the country. Everywhere they saw remains of the architecture of earlier ages which had been used in the construction of the modern houses. This was also the case in Gaza, the ancient town of the Philistines, which the small caravan reached on 19. March. Ancient capitals and fragments of granite and marble pillars decorated the lintels of the doors and windows of the houses. In the mosque they discovered two rows of columns of grey granite which must have come from a Roman temple.

Gaza had 4000 inhabitants in those days of whom 500 were Christians. The population was suffering at the time because of a programme of conscription. The years of tension between the power-hungry governor of Egypt, Mehmet Ali, and the Sultan in Istanbul had culminated that year in a regular outbreak of war in Palestine. Beasts of burden were being snatched everywhere for service in the army and our travellers were only able to find five camels, just enough for their luggage, to continue their journey. This meant they had to continue north on foot, being passed on the way by marching troops: «On loudly neighing horses, the glitter of arms,

Jaffa, in the foreground Polish Jews waiting for their ship after a pilgrimage to Jerusalem

24

Bethlehem, Church of the Nativity, Grotto of the Nativity

the trumpets sounding; and long lances with their glancing points and gay pennons appearing here and there among the trees, as they wound through the narrow lanes that divide the gardens, and led the thoughts back to the chivalry of older times.... groups of women collected on the high bank above the road; mothers and wives, met to take a last parting look, perhaps, of those most dear to them; and hands were raised and blessings loudly invoked as each familiar face was recognized in the passing ranks.»

The next stages of their journey were Ashkalon, so reminiscent of the crusades (after all, the English King Richard the Lionheart beat Sultan Saladin here in 1191), Ekron, Ashdod and Jaffa, situated on a hill 45 metres above the sea and surrounded by orange groves separated by hedges of prickly pear. It was reported that the quarantine had been lifted in Jerusalem so Roberts decided to go and visit the city while Kinnear set off straight for Beirut, where he had business to attend to. On 27. March Roberts and Pell set off with their servants. They rode through sweet-smelling orange groves on the edge of the fertile Sharon Plain. Roberts: «Not since I was a child have I felt such perfect pleasure in the beauties of Nature. This cheerfulness of spirit is only possible, I believe, if one has entered this wonderful country from the desert. The ground is carpeted with flowers... the plain is dotted with little villages, here and there there are groups of palm trees. The Judaean mountains form a magnificent backcloth and behind them lies the great city.»

In spite of information to the contrary the plague was still rampant in Jerusalem, as it had been for almost a year now. This could not, however, stop Roberts from entering the town: «My good sense may well whisper in my ear that it would be wiser to forego it (the visit).. but I am helpless against this long-felt desire; I simply must see this great city . . .» And, indeed, the quarantine was lifted on the morning of the day Roberts entered Jerusalem (29. March).

It was shortly before Easter and there were thousands of pilgrims in the city. The two men only managed to find somewhere to stay with the help of an acquaintance they had made in Hebron. On Palm Sunday they paid the governor, Achmed Aga, a formal visit and he invited them to accompany him when he led the pilgrims to their ritual bathe in the River Jordan a few days later.

After an unsatisfactory excursion to Jericho – which had not yet been excavated – they joined the governor's colourful cavalcade: «As we approached the river there was a great deal of pushing and shoving. The women started to shout with pleasure, a sound we had often heard in Egypt . . . Although the camels were heavily burdened they seemed to quicken their pace and their Arab riders could scarcely hold them back. The governor's rugs were spread out high on the bank above the river, where we could get a very good view of everything that went on. We sat on the left of the governor, surrounded by the military band and standard bearers.» To every-

Tyre with the causeway between the island city and the mainland

26

Sidon, looking towards the Lebanon

one's horror a young Greek, the person chosen for the special honour of being the first to be plunged into the choppy water, was drowned.

They continued their journey to the Dead Sea, to the oasis of Ein Gedi, which is famous for its dates, to the ancient convent of Mar Saba, where Roberts was allowed to draw in the chapel even though many devout pilgrims were at their Easter prayers, to Bethlehem, the town of King David and the place where Jesus was born. John Pell and Hanafi Ismail, who had acted as their interpreter so far, left him in Bethlehem to go back to Cairo via Al Arish. Roberts returned to Jerusalem with his Egyptian servant where he met an acquaintance from Cairo who accompanied him on the rest of his journey.

On 15. April they set off for Nablus near the Biblical town of Sichem, where Abraham is said to have entered the Promised Land and set up an altar; it later became a centre of the Samaritans, some three hundred of whom still lived there. The old tensions between this mixed race of Israelites and Assyrian colonists on the one hand and the rest of the Jews on the other were still to be noticed when they visited the Samaritan synagogue and the Rabbi stared at their Jewish guide with eyes full of hate.

They continued their journey through the fertile plain of Jesreel to Galilee where they visited, among other places, Nazareth – the town where Jesus spent his childhood and youth – and the Sea of Galilee. In Cana they were shown «the well at the entrance to the

27

village out of which had been drawn the water» that Jesus turned into wine at a wedding in the town.

They reached Akko on 23. April. It is an old port on the Mediterranean which, under the name of Saint Jean d'Acre, played quite an important role in the crusades; for a time it was even the capital of the Kingdom of Jerusalem. After a visit to Mount Carmel they again turned northwards. The next stages on their journey were the old island town of the Phoenicians, Tyre, whose merchants some three thousand years previously had founded colonies all around the Mediterranean (Carthage) as far as the south of Spain. Roberts particularly liked Sidon, once the rival of Tyre. From there they set off to cross the Lebanon using an old Roman road. It was cold and it was raining. One night one of their donkeys was attacked and wounded by a hyena; it took a great deal of loud shouting and heavy gunfire to chase the animal away. The next day they arrived in the fertile plain of Bika between the Lebanon and the anti-Lebanon on the northern edge of which Baalbek, their next destination, was situated.

Baalbek, entrance to the Temple of Bacchus with one of the blocks loosened in an earthquake

It was still pouring down, the ground was gradually turning into a morass and the peaks of the mountains on either side of the wide valley were covered with snow. It took them three days to reach Baalbek. They pitched their tents as well as they could. Their situation «was altogether a miserable one . . . The bedding and everything else was wet . . . after a quick meal I was glad to lie down again as I had felt ill the whole day.» During the night the tent collapsed under the weight of the water that had collected in a dip in the roof and the deluge went all over the sleeping men. In the morning they took refuge in a cow-byre. Although it rained the whole day and Roberts began to run a temperature he still visited the impressive ruins of the Roman Temple of the ancient city of Heliopolis, as Baalbek was called by the Greeks. His temperature rose in the afternoon and he became so exhausted he was forced to lie down again. During his three or four days in Baalbek he still managed to make at least seven drawings, among them the one of the entrance to the Temple of Bacchus which, when done in oil on his return to England, was the reason he was elected to the Royal Academy.

His health was so bad by this time that he gave up all his other plans and set off for Beirut on 8. May, from where he took a ship to Alexandria and from there via Malta and Gibraltar to London, which he finally reached on 21. July, 1839, after a long and difficult voyage. Sitting in his tent in the mountains during the night he had written in his diary: «This is probably the last night I shall spend in my tent, a fact which does not sadden me -and yet I feel something like the pangs of parting, parting from an old friend, my companion in the desert.» And he later wrote to a friend: «It is the most independent way of life imaginable, there are no bills to pay, there's no waiter waiting to be tipped – at dawn the tents are merely struck, the camels loaded up and off one sets for new, interesting destinations.»

The following coloured plates (most of which appeared in the first volume of his works) show just how great an impression the Holy Land made on Roberts, a painter who was highly esteemed during his lifetime and who died in 1864. This collection of paintings is almost complete and has seldom been printed, in such a large format, since the first publication.

The Colour Plates

Jerusalem, the Damascus Gate

Jerusalem, Church of the Holy Sepulchre, the Greek Orthodox Chapel

Jerusalem seen from the road to Bethania

Jerusalem, entrance to the Tombs of the Kings

Jerusalem, the Temple Mount with the Dome of the Rock

Kidron Valley, Tomb of Zacharias

Jerusalem from the South

Church of the Holy Sepulchre

Jerusalem. Church of the Holy Sepulchre

Jerusalem, Bethesda Pool between the Temple Mount (left) and St. Anna

41

Citadel of Jerusalem without the walls

Jerusalem, the Citadel

Jerusalem, the Golden Gate

View across the Kidron Valley to the Temple Mount

Kidron Valley, Shiloach tunnel

Jerusalem from the Mount of Olives

Jerusalem, Church of the Holy Sepulchre, Anointing Stone

CRYPT of the Holy Sepulchre
Jerusalem

Jerusalem Church of the Holy Sepulchre crypt

Hinnom Valley, Job's Well

Jerusalem from the North

Kidron Valley, Shiloach Pool

Jerusalem, entrance to the Citadel

Kidron Valley, Absalom's Tomb

Jerusalem, site of the Crucifixion in the Church of the Holy Sepulchre

Mount Tabor seen from the plain of Jesreel

Nazareth

Nazareth, Mary's Well

Nazareth, Franciscan monastery

Nazareth, Church of the Annunciation, Grotto of the Annunciation

Nazareth, (old) Church of the Annunciation

Cana, the well

David ROBERTS. R.A.

Tiberias on the Sea of Galilee, looking towards the Lebanon

David Roberts. R. A.

The Sea of Galilee with Tiberias